CW0048485S

Learn French
Like a Native
for Beginners
- Level 1

Learning French in Your Car Has Never Been Easier! Have Fun with Crazy Vocabulary, Daily Used Phrases, Exercises & Correct Pronunciations

LEARN LIKE A NATIVE

www.LearnLikeNatives.com

Table of Contents

Introduction

Benefits of Learning French

It is easy to stick with your native tongue. As an English speaker, you may feel that you have a considerable advantage. But are you not fascinated by other languages? By different cultures? Do you not find them captivating?

Let's say you are going to your holiday destination (maybe France, or even just a French-speaking country). Did you think of everything? First aid kit, papers, and documents? Very good, but what about your foreign language skills? Have you ever thought about how you will express yourself? Unfortunately, many travelers neglect this topic and believe that, with English, you can get anywhere. Some also assume you can communicate well with your hands and feet. The question you should ask yourself, though, is:

What do I expect from my journey, and which goals do I have (besides just relaxing, of course)?

To give you a little motivation, here are five advantages of being able to express yourself in the language of the country you are in:

- You get to know the locals much more authentically
- You understand the culture and attitude of people much better
- You can negotiate more effectively
- You do not waste valuable time, because you can communicate faster
- You feel safer

Just to keep it short, you do not have to learn a foreign language to perfection.

A Bit of History About This Beautiful Language...

French is a poetic language. There's something about the way the string of words sounds like. It is as if it is meant to woo a lover.

You may then be surprised to discover that French was actually derived from Vulgar Latin, the kind spoken by Roman soldiers. By 200 BC, this form of Latin became more popular and widespread throughout the Empire. Vulgar Latin gave birth to French and other romantic languages we know today - Italian, Spanish, Romanian, and Portuguese.

The Perfect Method

I'm sure you've been told there's no right or wrong way to learn a language. Well, that can't be right, because it's wrong! The truth is, most people don't lack in motivation, drive, excitement, determination, or even talent. More than anything, people lack the correct method.

I've been learning and teaching languages my whole life, and I've realized that the number one reason why people get stuck learning any language is simple. It's not because they are lazy, it's not because they don't have time, it's because they are bored!

You could go to the best schools and have the best teachers in the world, but if you're bored in your Spanish class, you're unlikely to get anywhere. Starting from scratch and ingesting new knowledge can be a daunting thing as it is. So, if you're not fully engaged, learning a new language will be a long road.

Think about it. You've been a child before. Did you learn grammar before you knew how to speak? Of course not! So why do that now? In my opinion, that's where most language methods fail. They get caught up in all the specific rules and formal details, before worrying about whether or not their students understand what's going on. What's the point in knowing irregular verbs, if you can't even order food at the restaurant! My point being, unless you're planning to write a Ph.D. in French, the most important thing for you is to be able to speak with other people.

That's where Learn Like A Native comes in!

With approximately 120 million people who speak and study French as a non-native language, there's plenty of opinions as to what the best way to learn is.

That's why I based my method on modern expert research. The latest studies show that the most efficient way to learn languages – and French in particular – is by learning vocabulary and grammar in conversation.

Using this method, I'll teach you how to apply formal knowledge in a real-life environment, through practical and relatable materials. With short and fun lessons, you'll stay engaged every step of the way, helping you retain vocabulary much more efficiently.

The audiobook version is narrated by a French native speaker who will get you comfortable with the sounds of the language. You'll take an active part in the learning process and be required to speak, repeat, and exercise new sounds as they come up throughout the lessons. If you have any trouble, the textbook will help you with written sounds so you can visualize letters and the sound they relate to.

You'll feel like you're in a French class. But one you can take everywhere! With only 20 to 30 minutes per lesson, you can focus on each topic independently without any stress. Squeeze them into your schedule, sitting in your car or waiting for the Bus, and enjoy the flexibility of going through each step at your own pace. No one is watching you, of course, but I trust you'll do the work!

Learning a new language is a complex and rich experience. After you are done with this book, you will be ready (or more prepared) to travel, immerse yourself in French-speaking cultures, read fiction and newspapers in French, watch films, eat French foods, learn recipes, make French-speaking friends and, most importantly, enjoy yourself!

This book is inspiring and vibrant to read and/or listen to, motivating you to speak and embrace the French language, no matter how new you are to it.Before you know it, you'll find yourself having a full-blown conversation in French and wonder how you got there!

Are you ready? Okay, then we can start. Whichever language level you achieve depends entirely on you.

FREE BOOK!

Get the *FREE BOOK* that reveals the secrets path to learn any language fast, and without leaving your country.

Discover:

- The **language 5 golden rules** to master languages at will

- Proven **mind training techniques** to revolutionize your learning

- A complete step-by-step guide to **conquering any language**

Chapter 1 – The first impression is very important

Everyone knows the old saying "you only get one chance to make a first impression."

Therefore, it's no surprise that one of the first things every child learns is to say hello and introduce themselves. Even J.K. Rowling, the famous author of that young wizard's adventures, said "A good first impression can work wonders", and I completely agree.

Just a simple "Hello" can make all the difference in a conversation. That's exactly the reason why we will begin this exciting adventure, learning greetings in French. You will learn how to introduce yourself and greet people at different times of the day, among other useful things.

We will start with the most popular greetings. There are several ways of greeting people in French, depending on who you are addressing and whether you want to be formal or not.

Ready to start? I really hope you are as excited as I am!

So, let's start with the most common ways to greet someone in French:

Hello.	Bonjour/Salut

Bon-joor – Sah-luh

The word "Bonjour" is probably one of the most popular French words and is now used as a friendly salutation around the world.

Salut, which is more informal, is also used quite often, but applies more to people you know personally, such as friends and family.

Good morning.	Bonjour

Translated literally, "Bonjour" means "good day". It is also used as a greeting upon waking up. You can use it in the morning and afternoon.

Contrary to English, the greetings don't change depending on the time of the day. As such, in the afternoon, you also say "Bonjour".

As the afternoon sets in, you should say "Good evening".

Good evening.	Bonsoir

Bon-swar

You can use this greeting on both formal and informal occasions. It is used both for when you are arriving and leaving a place.

Finally, at bedtime, you will say:

Good night.	Bonne nuit

Boh-nuh nu-ee

Remember! You should use "Bonne nuit" only when you are saying goodbye late at night. It is also used to wish sweet dreams.

Last one. When departing, you say:

Goodbye.	Au revoir / Ciao

Au revoir – Tchah-oh

You should remember that, depending on whether you are greeting a friend or a stranger, you would use a different salutation.

For example, when leaving a restaurant (or in any other formal occasion), you will say "Au revoir" if you want to sound polite. Although, you can use "Ciao" if you are saying goodbye to some old friends or to someone you know well (informal occasion).

Farewell.	Adieu
Farewell. I love you.	**Adieu**. Je t'aime

Ah-dee-euh

"Adieu" is used as a final salutation when you are pretty sure you are not going to see someone ever again. It's a phrase very rich in drama, sadness, or irony.

There is also a more informal version of "Au revoir"

See you later.	A plus tard.
Great! **See you later.**	Parfait! **À plus tard.**

Ah-plu-tar

How is your pronunciation? Hope you are starting to make progress.

| See you in a few. | À tout à l'heure |
| **Ok! See you in a few.** | Ok! **À tout à l'heure.** |

A-toot-a-leur

When greeting, you may also want to ask how someone is doing.

| How are you? | Comment ça va? / ça va? |

Ko-man-sah-vah

Asking "Comment ça va?" is a really good way to start a friendly conversation. It is an informal greeting and can also be used between people you are familiar with to ask about their health or mood. You can also simply say: ça va? There is no big difference between the two. Here's the literal translation of both expressions:

-Comment ça va? "How are you doing?"
-ça va? Are you alright/Are you okay?

| How can I help you? | Comment je peux t'aider? |

Koh-man-guh-puh-teh-deh

At this point, you have probably figured out the connection between two words: "how" and "comment", and you know how important the word "how" is in any language.

Let's see another sentence that uses the word "Comment":

What is your name?	Comment tu t'appelles?

Ko-man-tah-pel-tu

To say what your name is in French you use:

My name is	Je m'appelle
My name is John.	**Je m'appelle** John.

Juh-ma-pell

I am	Je suis
I am new around here.	**Je suis** nouveau ici.

Juh-suee

Thanks/Thank you.	Merci

Mer-see

"Merci" is used to say both "thanks" or "thank you". However, if you wish to show more gratitude, you could say "Thanks a lot" which translates to "Merci beaucoup".

Mer-see-bo-koo

I am sorry.	Je suis désolé.

Juh-suee-dé-zo-lé

Nice to see you again.	Ravi de te revoir.

Ra-vee-duh-tuh-ruh-vwar

Was it too hard? Don't worry. Greetings are basic phrases you will need to memorize, but I promise that following sentences will be shorter and easier to remember.

What is new?	Quoi de neuf?

Kwa-duh-neuf

Another sentence with similar meaning is "Qu'est-ce que tu racontes?" What do you say?

Ke-suh-kuh-tu-ra-ko-ntuh

How are you doing?	Comment vas-tu? Comment ça va?

Ko-man-va-tu

As you might know, "Ok" is an English expression. Nevertheless, it's universally used worldwide, even among French speakers. You should be aware, however, that there is a French equivalent:

Ok.	D'accord

Da-kor

How is it going? Is it easy? Or maybe you need to practice a little bit more. Practice is the key to mastery. Anyway, before we move to another topic, let's take a look at a short conversation that uses some of the words we have just learned.

You'll now listen to a short dialog between John and a Vendor.

You'll listen to the sentences, first in English and then in French.

Vendor   *Good morning!*

(Vendeur):   Bonjour

John: *Good morning to you, too.*

Bonjour à vous.

Vendor: *How can I help you?*

Comment puis-je vous aider?

John: *I am here to pick up a cake.*

Je suis ici pour récupérer un gâteau.

Vendor: *Sure. What is your name?*

Bien-sûr. Quel est votre nom?

John: *My name is John Hill.*

Je m'appelle John Hill.

Vendor: *Oh, I am sorry. Your bday cake is not ready yet.*

Oh, je suis désolé. Votre gâteau d'anniversaire n'est pas encore prêt.

John: *Ok. When can I come pick it up?*

D'accord. Quand est-ce que je peux venir le récuperer?

Vendor: *It will be ready in one hour.*

Ce sera prêt dans une heure.

John: *Great. I will run some errands and come back.*

Super. Je vais faire quelques courses et je reviens.

Vendor: *Thanks for understanding. See you in a few.*

Merci de votre compréhension. A tout à l'heure.

John: *Sure. See you later!*

Bien-sûr. A plus tard!

I hope John is not getting low blood sugar, because he will have to wait for a while. In the meantime, shall we go and learn some new words and phrases that relate to family and relatives? This could be really handy if you are going to celebrate your birthday!

Chapter 2 – Are we related?

I am sure your family would be pleased to tell you the story of your first word.

Language acquisition starts with receptive language, the understanding of sounds and words of the world around us. There is a good chance that either "mum" or "dad" (or a variable of these) was the first word you learned.

Dad	Papa
My **dad** went out to get more ice.	Mon **papa** est sorti chercher plus de glace.

Pah-pah

In the French language, usually the last syllable of each rhythmic group inside the sentence is pronounced at a higher pitch than the rest of the sentence. Here, we'll put the accent on the last « a ». Pah-pah

Mom	Maman
My **mom** is there, by the corner.	Ma **maman** est là-bas, vers le coin.

Mah-man

Son	Fils
My **son** used to play tennis.	Mon **fils** jouait au tennis avant.

Fiss

Daugther	Fille
My daughter likes to dance.	Ma **fille** aime danser.

Fee-yuh

Unlike English, French nouns have a gender *(genre):*

They can be masculine *(masculin)* or feminine *(féminin).* There are different ways to find out a noun's gender: we can look in the dictionary and check for the abbreviations *m. (masculine)* or *f. (feminine);* we can check the noun's ending, which generally gives an indication whether the noun is masculine or feminine; or we can look at the noun's article.

Nouns with the article *le* or *un* are masculine, and nouns with *la* or *une* are feminine. You should always learn nouns together with their articles to be sure of their gender.

Notice the difference between "mon" and "ma", both meaning "my".

In fact, "mon" is used for "my son", which is a masculine word. For "my daughter", which is a feminine word, we'll use "ma".

Brother	Frère
This is my **brother** Alex.	Voici mon **frère** Alex.

Freh-ruh

Sister	Soeur
She is my **sister** Coreen.	Elle, c'est **ma soeur** Coreen.

Suhr

Uncle	Oncle
I have two **uncles**.	J'ai deux **oncles.**

On-k-luh

Aunt	Tante

My **aunt** has two kids.	Ma **tante** a deux enfants.

Tan-tuh

- Most French nouns also form their plural by adding an **-s** to their singular form. But remember, this **-s** is always silent

Cousin	Cousin
My cousin lives far from here	Mon **cousin** vit loin d'ici.

Koo-zen

This one's easy to remember! It's the same word with a different pronounciation.

Grandfather	Grand-père
My **grandpa** picks up mangoes every day.	Mon **grand-père** cueille des mangues tous les jours.

Gran-peh-ruh

Grandmother	Grand-mère

| My **grandma** loved knitting. | Ma **grand-mère** adorait tricoter. |

Gran-peh-ruh

How is it going so far? Don't you worry, we just need to meet few more people, and then we can take a short break.

| Siblings | Frères/Soeurs |
| I have three **siblings**. | J'ai trois **frères/soeurs**. |

Freh-ruh/ Su-uhr

| Parents | Parents |
| I love my **parents**. | J'aime mes **parents**. |

Pah-ran

| Family | Famille |
| My **family** is big. | J'ai une grande **famille**. |

Fah-meey

| Neighbor | Voisin |
| Dan is a great **neighbor**. | Dan est un **voisin** super. |

Vwa-zen

Are you ready to use the words you just learned? Great!

Let's listen to a short conversation.

You'll listen to the sentences, first in English and then in French.

Allyson:	*Happy birthday!*
	Joyeux anniversaire!
Kelly:	*Hello! Thanks a lot! I am happy that you came.*
	Salut! Merci beaucoup! Je suis contente que tu sois venue.
Allyson:	*I am happy that you invited me.*
	Je suis contente que tu m'aies invitée
Kelly:	*Sure. Let me show you who everyone is.*

Bien-sûr. Laisse moi te montrer qui est qui.

Allyson: *Great!*

Super!

Kelly: *That girl is my sister, and my cousin John is sitting next to her.*

Cette fille est ma soeur, et mon cousin John est assis à côté d'elle.

Allyson: *Yeah. Next to them is your brother Mark, right?*

Oui. A côté d'eux c'est ton frère Mark, c'est ça?

Kelly: *Perfect! Yes. He picks me up sometimes.*

Parfait! Oui. Il vient me chercher parfois.

Allyson: *I remember.*

Je me souviens.

Kelly: *Good. By that other corner are grandma, grandpa and uncle Ed.*

Bien. Vers là-bas. Il y a ma grand-mère, mon grand-père et mon oncle Ed.

Allyson: *Your grandma looks so young!*

Ta grand-mère a l'air tellement jeune!

Kelly: *Yes. I hope I have the same luck.*

Oui. J'espère que j'aurais la même chance.

Allyson: *Don't we all?*

On l'espère tous, non?

Kelly: *Let's see... who's missing? Oh, well. Dad is outside,* *with the neighbors and the rest of the family.*

Voyons voir... Qui manque? Ah, oui. Mon père est dehors avec les voisins et le reste de la famille.

Allyson: *Great! I can't wait to meet them.*

Super! J'ai hâte de les rencontrer.

So, what do you think? Learning a new language is about listening to things over and over again and repeating many times. My advice is to always say the words out loud when practicing, so you should be able to see significant improvement moving on the next chapters.

Chapter 3 – What day is it?

Learn how to measure and tell the time is hugely important. In many cultures, punctuality is extremely important and viewed as a form of respect, and I personally think it is a great sign of courtesy. Of course, you will also learn the days of the week and months, so you can make plans. Another thing you may want to know when traveling abroad is what season is it, to know how to dress accordingly.

Second	Seconde
One minute has sixty **seconds**.	Une minute équivaut à soixante **secondes**.

Seh-gon-duh

Minute	Minute
One hour has sixty **minutes**.	Une heure équivaut à soixante **minutes**.

Mee-nu-tuh

Hour	Heure
There are twenty-four **hours** in a day.	Il y a vingt-quatre **heures** dans une journée.

Eu-ruh

Great, let's carry on.

Day	Jour
January has thirty-one **days**.	Il y a trente-et-un **jours** en Janvier.

Joor

Week	Semaine
We have one **week** to finish.	Nous avons une **semaine** pour terminer.

Suh-main-uh

Month	Mois
We will be there next **month**.	Nous serons là le **mois** prochain.

Mwah

Year	Année
One more birthday, one more **year**.	Un anniversaire de plus, une **année** de plus.

Ah-neh

Decade	Décennie
This **decade** is going to end soon.	Cette **décennie** va bientôt se terminer.

Deh-seh-nee

Century	Siècle
This is the discovery of the **century**.	C'est la découverte du **siècle**.

See-eh-kluh

Morning	Matin
The meeting was this **morning**.	La réunion était ce **matin**.

Mah-ten

Afternoon	Après-midi

Will you be there in the **afternoon**?	Tu seras là cet **après-midi**?

Ah-preh-mee-dee

Night	Nuit
The Moon comes out at **night**.	La lune sort la **nuit.**

Nu-ee

Spring	Printemps
Everything flowers in **spring**.	Tout fleurit au **printemps**.

Pren-tam

Summer	Eté
We had a fun **summer**.	Nous avons eu un **été** divertissent.

Eh-teh

Autumn	Automne
Look at the first **autumn** leaf.	Regardes la première feuille d'**automne**.

Oh-to-nuh

Winter	Hiver
W**inter** is here.	l'**hiver** est arrivé.

Ee-ver

January	Janvier
January is the first month of the year.	**Janvier** est le premier mois de l'année.

Jan-vee-eh

February	Février
That tree flowers in **February**.	Cet arbre fleurit en **Février**.

Feh-vree-eh

March	Mars
March is a good month for harvesting.	**Mars** est un bon mois pour la récolte.

Mars

April	Avril

| We stop activities in **April**. | Nous arrêtons les activités en **Avril**. |

Ah-vreel

Have you noticed how most of the names of the months are similar between English and French? That's a relief, isn't it?

May	Mai
May is going to be a great month.	**Mai** va être un mois super.

Meh

June	Juin
The break starts in **June**.	Les vacances commencent en **Juin**.

Ju-ein

July	Juillet
July is a hot month in France.	**Juillet** est un mois chaud en France.

Ju-ee-yeh

August	Août

This **August** will be rainy.	Ce mois d'**Août** sera pluvieux.

Ah-oo-t

September	Septembre
Next semester starts in **September**.	Le prochain semestre commence en **Septembre**.

Sep-ten-bruh

October	Octobre
My birthday is in **October**.	Mon anniversaire est en **Octobre**.

Ok-to-bruh

November	Novembre
We celebrated Halloween all **November**.	Nous avons célébré Halloween tout le mois de **Novembre**.

Noh-vem-bruh

December	Décembre

| Year ends in **December**. | L'année se termine en **Décembre**. |

Deh-cem-bruh

| Monday | Lundi |
| Today is **Monday**. | Aujourdhui, c'est **Lundì**. |

Leun-dee

| Tuesday | Mardi |
| I have an appointment for next **Tuesday**. | J'ai un rendez-vous pour **Mardì** prochain. |

Mar-dee

| Wednesday | Mercredi |
| **Wednesday** is not a good day for me. | **Mercredi** n'est pas un bon jour pour moi. |

Mer-kruh-dee

| Thursday | Jeudi |
| I'll see you next **Thursday**. | Je vous verrai **jeudi** prochain. |

Juh-dee

Friday	Vendredi
The party is next **Friday**.	La fête est **Vendredi** prochain.

Ven-druh-dee

Saturday	Samedi
I play every **Saturday**.	Je joue tous les **Samedis**.

Sah-muh-dee

Sunday	Dimanche
We can have lunch this **Sunday**.	Nous pouvons déjeuner ensemble ce **Dimanche**.

dDee-man-shuh

How is it going? Are you ready for a short dialogue?

Ally: *So, what are your plans for next year?*

Alors, quels sont tes plans pour l'année prochaine?

Juan: *I honestly don't know what will happen after winter.*

Sincèrement, je ne sais pas ce qui va se passer après l'hiver.

Ally: *Will you at least come back in February? The spring is lovely here.*

Tu pourras au moins revenir en Février? Le printemps est superbe ici.

Juan: *If I don't, I promise I will be back to celebrate summer, in July.*

Si je ne reviens pas, je promets que je serais là en Juillet, pour célébrer l'été.

Ally: *Everyone loves summer. I love autumn.*

Tout le monde adore l'été. Moi j'adore l'automne.

Juan: *Why?*

Pourquoi?

Ally: *Leaves change colors and I love the weather between September and November.*

Les feuilles changent de couleur et j'adore le climat entre Septembre et Novembre.

Juan: Two weeks ago you didn't love in it that much.

Il y a deux semaines tu n'aimais pas tellement ça.

Ally: Are you talking of that rainy Wednesday? I hated that.

Tu parles de ce mercredi pluvieux? J'ai détésté.

Juan: Yeah. As if it was not enough with those boring Mondays.

Oui. Comme si ces lundi ennuyants n'étaient pas assez.

Ally: Oh, sure. I don't like Mondays. I love Fridays.

C'est sur. Je n'aime pas les lundis. J'adore les vendredis.

Juan: Like everyone. But I like Saturdays better.

Comme tout le monde. Mais je préfère les samedis.

Ally: Yes. Especially the ones in Spring, when you take your boat for a ride.

Oui. Surtout au printemps. Quand tu peux prendre ton bâteau pour faire un tour.

Juan: You remember it. Good.

Tu t'en souviens. Super.

It is not as hard as you thought, right? There is a lot to remember, but sometimes it's easier if you find the similarities between English and French, as some in the names of the months. And let us repeat, practice makes perfect.

Now has come the time to learn some important verbs and how to conjugate them.

Chapter 4 – There is no gift like the Present

Just as in any other language, in French, verbs are an important part of everyday speaking. When studying a foreign language, the present is the first tense you learn as this allows you to form simple sentences. It is used to describe something that is happening right now or a state of being. Using the present tense, you will be able to speak about your desires, interests and plans.

First of all, in French, verb conjugation is done by changing the ending of the verb. Verbs are divided into 3 different categories of verbs, called "conjugations" – as in English. Each one is characterized by a specific ending in its infinitive form:

- First conjugation: Verbs ending in -ER (like aimer)
- Second conjugation: Verbs ending in -IR (like dormir)
- Third conjugation: Verbs ending in -RE (like croire)

In this chapter, I will teach you how to conjugate the regular verbs.

41

Hopefully, with a bit of practice, you will realize that French verb conjugation is actually much easier than it seems.

So, let's get started. There is no time like the present!

To love	Aimer	Root	Termination
I love	J'aime		ER changes for "e"
You love	Tu aimes		ER changes for "es"
He/She loves	Il/Elle aime		ER changes for "e"
We love	Nous aimons	Aim-	ER changes for "ons"
You love	Vous aimez		ER changes for "ez"
They love	Ils/Elles aiment		ER changes for "ent"

The root of all regular verbs never changes. As you can see, the root is the part preceding the infinitive ending. So, for example, in "Aimer" the root is "Aim-". As we said, the root always remains the same and different endings are added to denote the person, number or tense. Let's look at some examples.

I love the rain.	J'aime la pluie.
She loves the music.	Elle aime la musique.
You love movies.	Tu aimes les films.
They love to play music.	Ils aiment jouer de la musique.

Great! Here is a tip: using the above table you will be able to conjugate every other regular verb that ends in "-ER", all you will have to do is add to the root the relevant ending, as we just did. Clearly, the same logic applies to verb of the second and third conjugation (-IR and -RE). That's good to know, right?

Here are a few more examples. For the verb "to sing" - "chanter", you can separate the root "Chant-", and all you will need to do is to add the correct ending, as previously explained. The root of the verb "to sleep" – "dormir" is "dor-", and of the verb "to sell" - "vendre", the root is "Vend-".

Let's exercise with a fundamental verb: finir. In this case, the root is "Fin-".

To finish	Finir	Root	Termination
I finish	Je finis		Ir changes for "s"
You finish	Tu finis		Ir changes for "s"
He/She finishes	Il/Elle finit	Fini-	Ir changes for "t"
We finish	Nous finissons		Ir changes for "ons"
You finish	Vous finissez		Ir changes for "ez"

They finish	Ils/Elles finissent		Ir changes for "ent"

So, anyhow, what do you like to do in your free time? What

I finish work at 5pm.	Je finis de travailler à 17h.
She finishes school early today.	Elle finit l'école tôt aujourd'hui.
He finishes building his house.	Il finit de construire sa maison.
They finish their meal.	Ils finissent leur repas.

are your interests? What are you passionate about? Come on, think about this for a moment. Verbs are important to discuss all of these things.

To believe	Croire	Root	Termination
I believe	Je crois	Cro-	RE changes for "is"

You believe	Tu crois		RE changes for "is"
He/She believes	Il/Elle croit		RE changes for "it"
We believe	Nous croyons		RE changes for "yons"
You believe	Vous croyez		RE changes for "yez"
They believe	Ils croient		RE changes for "ient"

Note that even though they are written differently, the 1st, 2nd, 3rd singular person, as well as the 3rd plural person, are pronounced the same. This applies to all French verbs. Isn't that amazing?

You believe in loyalty.	Tu crois en la loyauté.
He believes in what he can touch.	Il croit en ce qu'il peut toucher.

| You believe in yourselves. | Vous croyez en vous-même. |
| They believe in you. | Ils croient en toi. |

The root of the verb "Croire" is "Cro-".

So, what have you learned, and what do you have faith in? Repeat with me: "Je crois....". Eventually, you will be able to better express yourself in French, but –in the meantime- "Je crois" is good enough.

Now let's look at the present of the auxiliary verb "to be" – "être". This verb is one of the most versatile and you will use it a lot in French, to introduce yourself, find out more about something or someone, describe places and things, etc. It is an auxiliary verb and its purpose is to help other verbs conjugate in compound tenses. In other words, it helps to create more complex sentences and tenses.

To be	**Être**
I am	Je suis
You are	Tu es

He/She/It is	Il/Elle est
We are	Nous sommes
You are	Vous êtes
They are	Ils sont

Alongside the verb "to be", "to have" – "avoir" – is the second most important verb in the French language. It is an auxiliary and irregular verb. It allows you to express numerous things: possessing something (literally or in a figurative way), communicate, express your needs and desires, etc.

To have	Avoir
I have	J'ai
You have	Tu as
He/She has	Il/Elle a
We have	Nous avons
You have	Vous avez

They have	Ils ont

I have a meeting at nine.	J'ai une reunion à neuf heures.
He has a television at home.	Il a une television à la maison.
We have a plan.	Nous avons un plan.
They have a place by the lake.	Ils ont une propriété près du lac.

Now let's see how the « présent progressif » - the present progressive – can help us.

The « présent progressif » could be compared to the present continuous in English. It forms with the verb to be in the present and the expression « en train de » + verb to infinitive.

The expression *être en train de* + infinitive verb is used to emphasize actions in progress, similar to the present progressive tense in English. These constructions take a conjugated form of the verb *être* (in the present) + *en train de* + inifinitive verb.

Unlike the simple present tense, which is sometimes used for actions in progress, *être en train de* never describes a regular or habitual action.

Examples:

What are you doing ? I'm working.	Tu fais quoi ? Je suis en train de travailler.
Have you finished writing the letter ? We are finishing.	Tu as fini d'écrire la lettre ? Nous sommes en train de finir.
Did he go to the grocery store? He is shopping right now.	Est-il allé au supermarché? Il fait les courses maintenant.
They are taking a test in classroom A.	Ils sont entrain de passer une évaluation dans la salle A.

Are you looking forward to putting this into practice?

Emma: *Hi. I am Emma.*

Salut. Je suis Emma.

David: *Nice to meet you. I am David.*

Enchanté. Je suis David.

Emma: *Tell me, David. What do you like to do?*

Dis moi, David. Qu'est-ce que tu aimes faire?

David: *I enjoy sailing on weekends.*

J'aime faire de la voile les weekends.

Emma: *Do you have a boat?*

Tu as un bâteau?

David: *Yes, I do. And what do you like to do?*

Oui, j'en ai un. Et qu'est-ce que tu aimes faire?

Emma: *I have a dancing academy. I love to teach.*

J'ai un club de dance. J'adore enseigner.

David: *Really? I have a niece. She loves to dance.*

Vraiment? J'ai une niece qui adore danser.

Emma: *Great! How old is she?*

Super! Elle a quel âge?

David: *She is 6 years old. Turns 7 in two weeks.*

Elle a 6 ans. Elle aura 7 ans dans deux semaines.

Emma: *I teach from 7. Maybe you could bring her. I am currently working on a ballet choreography.*

J'enseigne à partir de 7 ans. Peut-être que tu pourrais l'amener. Je suis en train de travailler sur une choréographie de ballet.

David: *Awesome. I am sure she will love it.*

Génial. Je suis sûr qu'elle va adorer.

As you can see, is very important to know how to conjugate the Present simple. Carry on with the practice until you achieve a better understanding.

Chapter 5 – Have a look around

Now, have a look around the room and tell me what you see. What is in the room? For instance, I usually keep a bottle of water on my desk, and I always carry my mobile phone and wallet. In this chapter, we will learn the names of a few things that you will probably have in your house.

Clock	Horloge
My **clock** says it is late.	Mon **horloge** indique qu'il est tard.

Or-loh-guh

Remember what we said at the beginning about punctuality? You will need a "horloge" to always be right on time.

Light	Lumière
Turn the **light** on.	Allume la **lumière.**

Luh-mee-eh-ruh

Money	Argent
Spend your **money** wisely.	Dépense ton **argent** de façon intelligente.

R-gan

Bed	Lit
This **bed** is comfortable.	Ce **lit** est confortable.

Lee

Window	Fenêtre
That **window** points south.	Cette **fenêtre** donne côté sud.

Fuh-neh-truh

Water	Eau
I want some **water**.	Je veux de l'**eau.**

oh

Car	Voiture
That is a nice **car.**	C'est une belle **voiture**.

Voo-ah-tur

Bicycle	Vélo
I took your **bicycle.**	J'ai pris ton **vélo**.

Veh-loh

Photo	Photo
I have your **photo** in my wallet.	J'ai ta **photo** dans mon porte-monnaie.

Foh-toh

News	Actualités
Did you read the **news**?	Tu as lu les **actualités**?

Ak-tu-ah-lee-the

"Les actualités" are very important to keep you informed.

Let me give you a little advice. When preparing to visit another country, you could start reading local news sources from that country a couple of weeks before you get there. That will give you an insight into what is happening in the country and – why not – also some great talking points when you are speaking with locals.

Bin	Poubelle
I put it all in that **bin**.	J'ai tout mis à la **poubelle**.

Poo-bel-uh

Toothbrush	Brosse à dents
I need a new **toothbrush**.	J'ai besoin d'une nouvelle **brosse à dents.**

Bross-ah-dan

Mirror	Miroir
That **mirror** looks dirty.	Ce **miroir** à l'air sale.

Mee-rwar

Laptop	Ordinateur portable
You can use my **laptop**.	Tu peux utliser mon **ordinateur portable.**

Or-dee-nah-tur por-tah-bluh

Computer	Ordinateur
That is my **computer**.	Ça, c'est mon **ordinateur**.

Or-dee-nah-tur

Cellphone	Téléphone portable
I don't find my **cellphone**.	Je ne trouve pas mon **portable**.

Por-tah-bluh

Id	Carte d'identité
Please, let me see your **id**.	Faites-moi voir votre **carte d'identité,** s'il-vous plaît.

Car-tuh dee-dan-tee-teh

Driving license	Permis de conduire
You look funny in your **license**.	Tu es marrant sur la photo de ton **permis de conduire.**

Per-mee duh con-duee-ruh

Wallet	Porte-monnaie
Did you find your **wallet**?	As-tu trouvé ton **porte-monnaie**?

Por-tuh-mo-neh

Are you ready to create your own list? How many of those things are there in your house? Ok, let us take an example to understand it better.

Nancy:	*Honey! Do you have everything you need for camp?*
	Chéri! Tu as tout ce dont tu as besoin pour la colonie?
Peter:	*Yes, mom. I think so.*
	Oui maman, je crois.
Nancy:	*Do you have your id and cellphone?*
	Tu as ta carte d'identité et ton portable?
Peter:	*Yes. I cannot find my toothbrush.*
	Oui. Je ne trouve pas ma brosse à dents.
Nancy:	*I saw it by the bathroom mirror.*
	Je l'ai vue près du miroir de la salle de bains.
Peter:	*Thanks! Can I bring my laptop?*

Merci! Est-ce que je peux amener mon ordinateur portable?

Nancy: *To camp? No! Bring your wallet. You need that.*

A la colonie? Non! Prends ton porte-monnaie.

Peter: *I need money, too.*

J'ai besoin d'argent, aussi.

Nancy: *It is on your bed.*

C'est sur ton lit.

Peter: *Good. I also need water and a small bin.*

Parfait. J'ai également besoin d'eau et d'une petite poubelle.

Nancy: *A bin? Why?*

Une poubelle? Pourquoi?

Peter: *For the food. Haven't you read the news? It's bear season.*

Pour la nourriture. Tu n'as pas lu les actualités? C'est la saison des ours.

Nancy: *Really? Ok. Keep your light close to you, just in case.*

Vraiment? Ok. Gardes la lumière près de toi, juste au cas ou.

Peter: *Sure. Thanks, mom.*

Bien-sûr. Merci, maman.

It is getting easier; I can feel it. I promise you that if you follow the instructions and keep repeating our little lessons, you will have great results. Feel free to go back to the previous chapters as many times as you like, and you will become fluent in no time!

If you need help to count how many times you are repeating a sentence, move on to the next chapter: we are going to learn numbers next!

Chapter 6 – How far can you count?

There are many nursery rhymes that help to introduce numbers even before a child understands numbers or how to count. It was probably through one of these songs that many of us learned numbers and measurements.

That is what we will learn in this chapter. Don't worry. You won't have to do any math!

When speaking in French, you will often need to use and understand numbers to express time, record dates and – of course – count. So here is a table to help you memorize them:

		Pronunciation
One	Un	Uhn
Two	Deux	Duh
Three	Trois	Troowa
Four	Quatre	Katr

Five	Cinq	Cenk
Six	Six	Sees
Seven	Sept	Set
Eight	Huit	Oo-eet
Nine	Neuf	Nuhf
Ten	Dix	Dis
Eleven	Onze	Onz
Twelve	Douze	Dooz
Thirteen	Treize	Trehz
Fourteen	Quatorze	Ka-toh-rz
Fifteen	Quinze	Kenz
Sixteen	Seize	Sez

As you can see, all the numbers from one to sixteen are specific words, and as such you will have to learn it by hear. From seventeen to nineteen, numbers are formed from the root "dix-") meaning ten.

Seventeen	Dix-sept	Dee-set
Eighteen	Dix-huit	Dee-zoo-eet
Nineteen	Dix-neuf	Dee-z-nuhf

All compound numbers are formed adding the ten and the unit. You could read these numbers as "ten eight", i.e. "Dix-huit".

The same goes for numbers from 21 to 29. We just take the root number (vingt) and add the unit.

Twenty	Vingt	Ven
Twenty one	Vingt-et-un	Ven-the-uhn
Twenty two	Vingt-deux	Ven-tuh-duh
Twenty three	Vingt-trois	Ven-troo-ah
Twenty four	Vingt-quatre	Vent-kah-truh
Twenty five	Vingt-cinq	Vent-senk

Twenty six	Vingt-six	Vent-sees
Twenty seven	Vingt-sept	Vent-set
Twenty eight	Vingt-huit	Vent-hueet
Twenty nine	Vingt-neuf	Vent-nuhf

Note how twenty-one is slightly different, as French people say "vingt-et-un", meaning "twenty-and-one". Same goes for thirty-one, forty-one etc... For the other numbers, the "and" is not used.

Thirty	Trente	Tran-tuh
Thirty one	Trente-et-un	Tran-teh-euhn
Thirty two	Trente-deux	Tran-tuh-duh
Fourty	Quarante	Kah-ran-tuh
Fifty	Cinquante	Sen-kan-tuh
Sixty	Soixante	Soo-ah-san-tuh
Seventy	Soixante-dix	Soo-ah-san-tuh dees

Eighty	Quatre-vingt	Kah-truh-ven
Ninety	Quatre-vingt-dix	Kah-truh-ven-this
One hundred	Cent	san
One thousand	Mille	Meel

Any non-native French person learning the language will agree that one of the trickiest things to get to grips with is the number system.

It might be smooth sailing until you get to sixty-nine, but then funny things start to happen because they don't have a separate word for seventy, or eighty, or even ninety for that matter.

Soixante-dix (70) literally means "sixty-ten," *soixante et onze* (71) means "sixty and eleven," *soixante-douze* (72) means "sixty-twelve," etc.

Likewise, there's no word for "eighty" in standard French.* The French say *quatre-vingts*, literally four-twenties.** So 81 is *quatre-vingt-un* (four-twenty-one), 82 is *quatre-vingt-deux* (four-twenty-two), etc.

In keeping with the general weirdness at this end of the number scale, there's no standard French word for ninety* either; it follows the same pattern as 70. That is, you continue using *quatre-vingt* and adding from ten. 90 is *quatre-vingt-dix* (four-twenty-ten), 91 is *quatre-vingt-onze* (four-twenty-eleven), etc.

In some French-speaking areas, such as Belgium and Switzerland, "seventy" is *septante* and "ninety" is *nonante*. As for 80, Belgium uses the standard *quatre-vingts*, while Switzerland uses *huitante*. There's also an archaic word *octante* that you might hear in Switzerland.

Let's move on to ordinal numbers. As the name suggests, they tell the "order" of things. These numbers show rank or position.

First	Premier	Pruh-mee-eh
Second	Second	Suh-guon
Third	Troisième	Troo-ah-zee-m
Fourth	Quatrième	Ka-tree-m
Fifth	Cinquième	Sen-kee-m
Sixth	Sixième	See-z-m

Seventh	Septième	Set-ee-m
Eighth	Huitième	Hueet-m
Nineth	Neuvième	Nuh-vee-m
Tenth	Dixième	Dee-zee-m

As is the case with cardinal numbers, each of the first ten ordinal numbers has a distinct form. Form eleventh onward, ordinal numbers are formed by dropping the final vowel of the number and adding the suffix –ième.

Eleventh	Onzième	Onz-ee-m
Twelfth	Douzième	Dooz-ee-m
Thirteenth	Treizième	Trez-ee-m
Fourteenth	Quatorzième	Ka-tor-zee-m
Fifteenth	Quinzième	Ken-zee-m
Twentieth	Vingtième	Ven-tee-m

Have you seen how easy it is to create ordinal numbers? I know it's not a competition, but why not try to get there first?

Chapter 7 – What did you want to be when you grew up?

W hat did you want to be when you grew up?" How many times did someone ask you this question when you were a child? And how many times have you changed your answer?

When I was little, I wanted to be a scientist. Later on, I wanted to be a singer. Nowadays, I am a writer, but previously I have had different jobs. I have been a teacher, an electrician – honestly, not a very good one- and a chef.

We always need to remember that all professions are important. We need farmers to produce food of the highest quality, doctors to treat injuries and disease, artists to represent the beauty of the world around us.

Speaking of artists, this is a good word to start with.

Artist	Artiste
Manet was an **artist.**	Manet était un **artiste.**

R-tees-tuh

You should always keep in mind that vowels like "a" are very open and clear in . "A" is pronounced like the English word "ah!". "Artiste"

Chef	Chef/ Chef de cuisine
I want to become a **chef**.	Je veux devenir un **chef de cuisine.**

Sh-eh-f

Construction worker	Ouvrier
My dad is a **construction worker**.	Mon père est un **ouvrier**.

Oo-vree-eh

Firefighter	Pompier
Being a **firefighter** is a risky job.	**Pompier** est un emploi risqué.

Pom-pee-eh

Doctor	Docteur
The **doctor** will see you in 5 minutes.	Le **docteur** vous reçevra dans 5 minutes.

Doc-tuh-r

Policeman	Policier
A **policeman** came to our house.	Un **policier** est venu à la maison.

Po-lee-see-eh

Teacher	Enseignant
That is my **teacher**.	Voici mon **enseignant**.

An-seh-nee-an

Actor/Actress	Acteur/Actrice
Emma Stone is an **actress**.	Emma Stone est une **actrice**.

Ac-trees

Banker	Banquier
I am waiting for a **banker**.	J'attends un **banquier**.

Ban-kee-eh

Butcher	Boucher

| I am calling the **butcher** to order. | J'appelle le **boucher** pour commander. |

Boo-sh-eh

| Dentist | Dentiste |
| I have a great **dentist.** | J'ai un **dentiste** formidable. |

Den-tees-tuh

| Driver | Conducteur |
| My **driver** is very fast. | Mon **conducteur** va très vite. |

Kon-duk-tuhr

Are you making any progress?

| Electrician | Electricien |
| You need to call the **electrician**. | Tu dois appeler l'**electricien**. |

Eh-lehk-tree-see-ehn

Farmer	Agriculteur
My grandpa was a **farmer**.	Mon grand-père était un **agriculteur**.

Ah-gree-cul-tuhr

Hairdresser	Coiffeur/Coiffeuse
I have a great **hairdresser**.	J'ai un excellent **coiffeur**.

Kwa-fuhr

Journalist	Journaliste
I will be a **journalist.**	Je serais un **journaliste**.

Joor-nah-lee-stuh

Lawyer	Avocat
My daughter is a **lawyer**.	Ma fille est une **avocate**.

Ahv-voh-ka-tuh

Painter	Peintre
That **painter** did a good job.	Ce **peintre** a fait un bon travail.

Pen-truh

There are plenty of professions but don't worry, we won't go through them all. Just a few more words.

Politician	Politicien
I want to be a **politician**.	Je veux être un **politicien**.

Po-lee-tee-see-en

Psychologist	Psychologue
I am a **psychologist**.	Je suis un **psychologue**.

Psee-ko-lo-guh

Scientist	Scientifique
Scientists are addressing climate change.	Les **scientifiques** s'intéressent au changement climatique.

See-an-tee-feek

What did you want to be when you grew up? Let's learn few more words.

Plumber	Plombier

| I have to call the **plumber.** | Je dois appeler le **plombier**. |

Ploh-meh-roh

| Secretary | Secretaire |
| My **secretary** is on vacation. | Ma **secrétaire** est en vacances. |

Suh-creh-ter

| Shoemaker | Cordonnier |
| The **shoemaker** did a good job. | Le **cordonnier** a fait du bon travail. |

Kor-doh-nee-eh

| Singer | Chanteur |
| She's a great **singer**. | Elle est une bonne **chanteuse**. |

Shan-tuh-zuh

| Waiter/Waitress | Serveur/Serveuse |

I'll call the **waiter**.	Je vais appeler le **serveur**.

Ser-vuhr

Writer	Ecrivain
It is hard to be a **writer**.	C'est difficile d'être un **écrivain**.

Eh-kree-vein

Translator	Traducteur
I work as a **translator**.	Je travaille en tant que **traducteur**.

Tra-duk-tuhr

Ready for a dialogue?

Cris:	*Hey! What do you have there?*
	Salut! Qu'est-ce que tu as là?
Layla:	*It's a firefighter costume.*
	C'est un costume de pompier

Cris: *Is November yet?*

On est déja en Novembre?

Layla: *No! My son's school is going to have a "career day".*

Non! L'école de mon fils organise une journée des métiers.

Cris: *Oh, I see. I wanted to be a psychologist when I was nine.*

Oh, je vois. Je voulais être un pychologue quand j'avais neuf ans.

Layla: *I wanted to be a teacher. We are always changing, right?*

Je voulais être enseignant. Nous changeons tout le temps d'avis, pas vrai?

Cris: *Yeah. I wanted to be a teacher when I was fourteen.*

Oui. Je voulais être enseignant quand j'avais quatorze ans.

Layla: *How did you decide to become a lawyer?*

Comment as-tu décidé de devenir avocat?

Cris: *Well... you know. I was seventeen and wanted to change the world.*

Ben... Tu sais. J'avais dix-sept ans et je voulais changer le monde.

Layla: *My son wants to be a farmer.*

Mon fils veut être agriculteur.

Cris: *Is his mother not a politician?*

Sa mère n'est elle pas politicienne?

Layla: *Yeah. She started as a journalist and then changed careers.*

Si. Elle a commence en tant que journaliste puis elle a changée de carrière.

Cris: *Indeed. We are always changing.*

C'est vrai. On change tout le temps.

Now, repeat with me: "I wanted to be" -"je voulais être" and complete the sentence.

One of the first questions people ask to someone they have just meet is "What is your job?" which translates to "Quel est ton métier?" Thanks to what we have just learned in this unit, you are going to be ready for this conversation!

What next? Let's go to learn how to give directions.

Chapter 8 – Where are we going?

B e able to clearly tell where you want to go is very important, especially when traveling in another country. For this reason, have the ability to communicate in simple situations such as asking for directions can make your life easier, in case of a SatNav failure or during a relaxing afternoon walk when you don't have your mobile with you.

Street	La rue
That is the main **street**.	C'est la rue principale.

ruh

Avenue	Avenue
This is Clemenceau **Avenue**.	Voici l'**Avenue** Clémenceau.

A-vuh-nu

Block	Quartier

We are going to the **block** party.	Nous allons à la fête du **quartier**.

Kar-tee-eh

Square	Place
The **square** shouldn't be far from here.	La **place** ne devrait pas être très loin.

Plah-ssuh

Building	Immeuble
This **building** has 110 floors.	Cet **immeuble** a 110 étages.

E-mub-luh

Monument	Monument
This **monument** is 300 years old.	Ce **monument** a 300 ans.

Moh-nuh-man

Hospital	Hopital
The **hospital** is 5 minutes away.	L'**hopital** est à 5 minutes d'ici.

Ho-p-tal

Corner	Angle
The store is passing that **corner.**	Le magasin est après cet **angle**.

An-gluh

Nearest	Le plus proche
That is the **nearest** mall.	Voici le centre commercial le **plus proche**.

Pluh-proh-shuh

Turn left	Tourner à gauche
You should **turn left** here.	Tu devrais **tourner à gauche** ici.

Toor-neh-ah-goh-shuh

Turn right	Tourner à droite
Let's **turn right** after this corner.	**Tournons à droite** à cet angle.

Toor-neh-ah-droo-what

Go straight on	Aller tout droit

You only have to **go straight** on and you will get there.	Tu dois seulement **aller tout droit** et tu y arriveras.

Ah-leh-too-droo-ah

Go past	Dépasser
You have to **go past** the main street.	Tu dois **dépasser** l'avenue principale.

Deh-pah-seh

Crossroads	Intersection
Take the left on the **crossroads**.	Prenez à gauche à l'**intersection**.

N-tehr-sec-see-on

Those phrases will take you wherever you desire! Are you ready to put into practice what we have just learned about directions?

John: *Hey, sir! Good afternoon.*

Bonjour, monsieur!

Vendor:
(Vendeur)

What can I do for you?

Que puis-je faire pour vous?

John:

Can you tell me how I can get to the train station?

Est-ce que vous pouvez me dire comment me rendre à la gare?

Vendor

Sure. You have to go in that direction for 300m.

Bien-sûr. Vous devez prendre cette direction pendant 300m.

John:

I have to go past the library?

Est-ce que je dois dépasser la bibliothèque?

Vendor

Yes. Then, you turn left and go for another five or six hundred meters.

Oui. Après, vous tournez à gauche et avancer encore cinq ou six-cent mètres.

John:

Oh, I think I come from there. But I got confused at the crossroads.

Oh. Je crois que je viens de là-bas. Mais j'étais confus à l'intersection.

Vendor   *Very usual. You have to take a left at the crossroads.*

C'est normal. Vous devez prendre à gauche à l'intersection.

John: *Ok.*

D'accord.

Vendor   *You will see a square. The station is in front.*

Vous verrez une place. La gare est en face.

John: *Thank you very much.*

Merci beaucoup.

Vendor: *Don't worry. Have a nice trip.*

Pas de problème. Bon voyage.

Are you ready to go and explore a new place? Better hurry! "Survival 101" is coming.

Chapter 9 – Survival 101

E ach chapter contains helpful information, but this is particularly important. We have already said that: things do happen. Your child may feel unwell, you could twist an ankle while hiking, lose your passport... things do happen. So it's better to be prepared, right?

I believe that this sentence in particular is fundamental for you:

Do you speak English?	Parlez-vous Anglais?

Par-leh-voo-an-gleh

That is a question you should always remember, as could make your life much easier.

Where is the bathroom?	Où sont les toilettes?

oo-son-leh-twah-let

How can I get to this place?	Comment puis-je me rendre à cet endroit?

Ko-man-puee-juh-muh-ran-druh-ah-set-an-droo-ah

Where is the nearest hospital?	Où se trouve l'hôpital le plus proche?

Oo-suh-troo-vuh-loh-pee-tal-luh-plu-proh-shuh

When is the next flight?	Quand est le prochain vol?

Kaan-eh-luh-proh-chen-vol

Who can I talk to about this problem?	A qui puis-je parler de ce problème?

Ah-kee-puh-ee-juh-par-leh-duh-suh-proh-blem

Where can I find a policeman?	Où est-ce que je peux trouver un policier?

Oo-eh-suh-kuh-juh-puh-troo-veh-un-poh-lee-cee-eh

Though I hope you will never need this:

Where is the embassy?	Où se trouve l'embassade?

oo-suh-troo-vuh-lam-bah-sah-duh

What do I need to visit...?	Qu'est-ce que je devrais visiter...?

Keh-suh-kuh-juh-duh-vreh-v-z-teh

Where can I find...?	Où puis-je trouver ...?

Oo-puee-juh-troo-veh

Oh, I really hope you won't need any of them. But better safe than sorry! Let's see a short dialogue now.

Harry: *Hello, sir. How can I get to Kapital Burger, in Clemenceau Avenue?*

Bonjour Monsieur. Comment puis-je me rendre au Kapital Burger, à l'avenue Clémenceau?

Driver: *I can take you, but it is far. Is someone waiting for you? It's rush hour.*

Je peux vous y amener, mais c'est loin. Quelqu'un vous attends? C'est l'heure de pointe.

Harry: *No. I think I left my passport there.*

Non. Je crois que j'ai laissé mon passeport là-bas.

Driver: *It will take us at least 40 minutes to get there.*

Ça nous prendra au moins 40 minutes pour y aller.

Harry: *Ok. Maybe I can talk to someone there.*

D'accord. Peut-être que je peux parler à quelqu'un là-bas.

Vendor: *Good afternoon. Kapital Burger.*

Bonjour. Kapital Burger.

Harry: *Hello! My name is Harry Klein. I was there last night, and I think I left my passport.*

Bonjour! Je m'appelle Harry Klein. J'ai dîné chez vous hier soir et je crois que j'ai laissé mon passeport.

Vendor: *One second, please. Do you remember where you were sitting?*

Une seconde, s'il vous plaît. Vous vous rappelez de l'endroit où vous étiez assis?

Harry: *Yes. I was at the bar, by the corner.*

Oui. J'étais au bar, dans l'angle.

Vendor: *Ok. Give me a second.*

D'accord. Donnez moi une seconde.

Harry: *Ok.*

Ok.

Vendor: *Yeah. I just consulted my coworkers and they did not find anything. I am sorry.*

Oui. Je viens de demander à mes collègues et ils n'ont rien trouvé. Je suis désolé.

Harry: *Thank you.*

Merci

Driver: *They didn't find it?*

Ils ne l'ont pas trouvé?

Harry: *No. Where is the nearest police station?*

Non. Où est le commissariat le plus proche?

Driver: *Don't you want to go to your embassy? Could be better.*

Vous ne voulez pas aller à votre embassade? Ce serait mieux.

Harry: *Oh, yes. Where's the UK embassy?*

Oh, oui. Où est l'embassade du Royaume-Uni?

Driver: *Actually, it is near from here. We will be there in a few minutes.*

C'est près d'ici. Nous y serons dans quelques minutes.

What a nightmare to lose your passport abroad! I sincerely hope you never have to use any of these phrases.

Now, let's move on to something less stressful. Shall we switch to colors?

Chapter 10 – What is the color of the sky?

I will tell you a secret: I love a wonderful view, and everywhere I go, I like just to lose myself gazing at the sky. I particularly love the sunset. I also like the sunrise, but I'm not really a morning person.

How many colors are there in the sky?

Yellow	Jaune
My dress is **yellow**.	Ma robe est **jaune**.

Joh-nuh

Blue	Bleu
The sky looks very **blue**.	Le ciel à l'air très **bleu**.

Bluh

Red	Rouge
I bought a **red** car.	J'ai acheté une voiture **rouge**.

Roo-guh

Purple	Violet
Those flowers are **purple.**	Ces fleurs sont **violettes**.

V-oh-let-uh

Pink	Rose
My daughter wants a **pink** skirt.	Ma fille veut une jupe **rose**.

Roh-suh

Green	Vert
The fields look very **green** this year.	Les champs ont l'air très **verts** cette année.

Ver

Orange	Organge
I want my **orange** t-shirt.	Je veux mon t-shirt **orange**.

Oh-ran-guh

Brown	Marron
Your dog is **brown.**	Ton chien est **marron**.

Mah-ron

Grey	Gris
Grey is a mixed color.	Le **gris** est une couleur mixte.

Gree

Black	Noir
Black is my favorite color.	Le **noir** est ma couleur préférée.

Noo-r

White	Blanc
I painted the walls **white**.	J'ai peint les murs en **blanc**.

Blan

Fun fact: black and white are not colors. They represent, respectively, the absence of light and the lack of shadow.

Let's look at an example.

Lisa: *Hey, honey! I need your help with something.*

Hey, chéri! J'ai besoin de ton aide avec quelque chose.

Alex: *Yes, love. What is it?*

Oui, mon amour. Qu'est-ce qu'il y a?

Lisa: *We need to pick the colors for the house before we move.*

Nous devons choisir les couleurs pour la maison avant le déménagement.

Alex: *Oh, true. What do you have in mind?*

Oh, c'est vrai. Qu'est-ce que tu as en tête?

Lisa: *I was thinking of a light blue for our room, with touches of yellow.*

Je pensais à du bleu clair pour notre chambre, avec des touches de jaune.

Alex: *Ok. What have you thought of the living room?*

D'accord. A quoi tu penses pour le salon?

Lisa: *I am thinking of a combination of red and white walls.*

Je pense à une combinaison de murs rouges et blancs.

Alex: *Do you think that my black chair will match?*

Tu penses que ma chaise noire ira bien avec ça?

Lisa: *Positive. And for the studio, I was looking for something more neutral.*

Certainement. Et pour le studio, je cherchais quelque chose de plus neutre.

Alex: *By neutral you mean...?*

Par neutre tu veux dire...?

Lisa: *Earth colors. Like a light brown.*

Des couleurs de la terre. Comme un marron clair.

Alex: *And the nursery?*

Et la chambre du bébé?

Lisa: *Grey, with a purple wall.*

Gris, avec un mur violet.

Alex: *It sounds amazing. Thanks for planning all this.*

Ça à l'air génial. Merci d'avoir pensé à tout ça.

Lisa: *Sure! I love it!*

Avec Plaisir! J'adore!

What about you? Are you already planning to repaint your whole house? And for your dining room, would you like to go and buy some lanterns at an artisanal market in Paris? Imagine all the things you could do! First of all, however, we need to get there. Shall we just do that?

Chapter 11 – So much to do, so much to see

Where do you dream of going? Personally, I love the mountains. I grew up in a village in the valley, with a stunning view of the mountains. I think maybe that's why I love mountains so much! But anyway, enough about me.

Now, imagine where you would like to go…

Travel	Voyager
She lost the scarf during her last **travel**.	Elle a perdu son echarpe lors de son dernier **voyage**.

Voo-ah-ya-guh

Ticket	Billet
I bought a two-way **ticket**.	J'ai acheté un **billet** aller retour.

B-eh

Airplane	Avion
This **airplane** is big.	Cet **avion** est grand.

Ah-v-on

Reservation	Réservation
He made a **reservation** for tonight.	Il a fait une **réservation** pour cette nuit.

Reh-zer-vah-see-on

Hotel	Hotel
I like this **hotel**.	J'aime bien cet **hotel**.

Ho-tel

Room	Chambre
They need a double **room**.	Ils ont besoin d'une **chambre** double.

Sham-bruh

Key	Clef
I lost my **key**.	J'ai perdu ma **clef**.

Kleh

Passport	Passeport
Can I see your **passport**?	Puis-je voir votre **passeport**?

Pah-spor

Taxi	Taxi
Let's take a **taxi.**	Prenons un **taxi.**

Tac-si

"Taxi" is the same both in French and in English.

Car rental	Location de voiture
Where is the **car rental**?	Où se trouve le bureau de **location de voiture?**

Loh-kah-see-on

Bus	Bus
We will take the **bus.**	Nous allons prendre le **bus.**

Bus

Subway	Metro

| The subway was out of service. | Le **metro** était hors service. |

Meh-troh

| Train | Train |
| I'll take the **train**. | Je prendrai le **train**. |

Tren

| Station | Station |
| That is the nearest **station**. | Voici la **station** la plus proche. |

Stah-see-on

| Theater | Théâtre |
| This **theater** was remodeled 5 years ago. | Ce **théâtre** a été reconstruit il y a 5 ans. |

Teh-ah-truh

| Beach | Plage |
| She wants to go to the **beach**. | Elle veut aller à la **plage**. |

Pla-guh

Mountain	Montagne
They want to climb that **mountain.**	Ils veulent grimper cette **montagne.**

Mon-ta-nee-uh

Island	Ile
Let's go to that **island**.	Allons sur cette **île**.

Eel

City	Ville
Canada has big **cities**.	Le Canada a des grandes **villes**.

Veel-luh

Are you ready? You know what's coming next!

Shaun: *I want to buy the tickets for our travel. Can we decide on something?*

Je veux acheter les billets pour notre voyage. On peut se mettre d'accord?

Vanessa: *Sure! Where do we want to go?*

Bien-sûr. Où est-ce qu'on veut aller?

Shaun: *Not another city. I want to rest.*

Pas encore une ville. Je veux me reposer.

Vanessa: *I agree. Do you remember that beautiful mountain that Lisa showed us? Navarino Island.*

Je suis d'accord. Tu te rappelles de cette montagne magnifique que Lisa nous a montrée? L'île de Navarino.

Shaun: *Oh, sure. That cozy mountain house, right?*

Ah, bien-sûr. La maison de montagne chaleureuse, c'est ça?

Vanessa: *Yes. That one.*

Oui. C'est ça.

Shaun: *That sounds great. Do you think it is available?*

Ça à l'air génial. Tu penses que c'est disponible?

Vanessa: *On it!*

Je suis dessus!

Shaun: *Remember to check for a view.*

Rappelles-toi de regarder s'il y a une vue.

Vanessa: *I got the perfect room! It is beautiful.*

J'ai trouvé la chambre parfaite! Elle est magnifique.

Shaun: *Great. I need our passports to buy the tickets. I'll go get them.*

Super. J'ai besoin de nos passeports pour acheter les billets. Je vais les chercher.

Vanessa: *Sure. I am excited!*

D'accord. Je suis super excitée!

So, are you getting excited?

Repeat with me: "je veux voyager –I want to travel-, and make it happen. Traveling is an amazing way to meet new people and discover beautiful places. In my opinion, traveling is growing up and you can never end it!

A spontaneous trip, a last-second vacation... these are usually the best things. These are the kind of stories you will remember forever. Some memories are just amazing!

And do you know what else I like when traveling? The food!

A Quick Message

A quick message before we start the final chapter of this book.

"No one can whistle a symphony. It takes a whole orchestra to play it." –

H.E. Luccock

Do you want to be part of the orchestra of the Learning Spanish community?

Here is how:

If you're enjoying this book, I would like to kindly ask you to leave a brief review on Amazon.

Reviews aren't easy to come by, but they have a profound impact in supporting my work. This way, I can keep creating new content to help the whole community at my very best.

I would be incredibly thankful if you could just take a minute to leave a quick review on Amazon, even if it's just a sentence or two!

It's that simple!

Thank you so much for taking the time to leave a short review on Amazon.

The community and I are very appreciative, as your review makes a difference.

Now, let's get back to learning Spanish!

Chapter 12 : I am a bit hungry

F rench people are known for their gastronomy and set amazingly high culinary standards. The French have been the leaders and are recognized as innovators in the culinary arts scene since the beginning of time.

Most of the famous chefs in history are French. We could cite a few such as Paul Bocuse, Joël Robuchon, or Anne-Sophie Pic. The well known and famous chefs that are not French, nevertheless, are mostly trained in the art of cooking « à la Française », the « French-style ». Cooking knowledge and skills required to prepare a good meal is something that the French people take excessive pride in when they present meals.

France has many culinary regions, and each one has a specific characteristic of its own food and area. Generally, French food requires the use of many different types of sauces and gravies. The northwestern region of France produces recipes for cuisine that tend to require ingredients like apples, milk, butter, and cream, and the meals tend to be extremely rich and sometimes rather heavy. Reminiscent of the German style of food, the southeastern area of France, the French cuisine is heavy in lard and meat products such as sauerkraut and pork sausage.

The more widely accepted type of French food is southern French Mediterranean cuisine. This type of food is often served in traditional French restaurants. The dishes are a lot lighter in fat in the southeastern area of France. In the southeast area of France, culinary creations tend to lean more toward the side of a light olive oil than any other type of oil and usually don't use butter. Also, they rely heavily on herbs and tomatoes, as well as tomato-based products.

Cooking is an essential part of French culture, like sharing a meal and a good bottle of wine. French people find quality time, good food, and drinks, really important.

Are you ready to practice?

Tomato	Tomate
You only need a few **tomatoes**.	Tu as seulement besoin de quelques **tomates.**

Toh-mah-tuh

This one is not that hard, right? You should know that tomatoes are used in a lot of Mediterranean dishes, so you might want to remember this one.

Corn	Maïs
I love **corn.**	J'adore le **maïs**.

Ma-ees

Egg	Oeuf
She wants **eggs** and ham.	Elle veut des **oeufs** et du jambon.

Jam-bohn

Cheese	Fromage
I don't eat **cheese**.	Je ne mange pas de **fromage**.

Froh-mah-guh

Cheese is also VERY important in the French culture.

Butter	Beurre
French people love **butter.**	Les français aiment le **beurre**.

Buh-rruh

Sandwich	Sandwich
We want five regular **sandwiches**.	Nous aimerions avoir cinq **sandwich** classiques.

Sand-weesh

Burger	Hamburger
They want three **burgers**.	Ils veulent trois **hamburgers**.

Ham-bur-gher

Salad	Salade
I want a Caesar **salad.**	Je veux une **salade** César.

Sa-lah-duh

Shrimp	Crevettes

It has **shrimps** inside.	Il y a des **crevettes** à l'intérieur.

Kruh-vet-uh

Sausage	Saucisse
We love **sausages** for breakfast.	Nous adorons la **saucisse** au petit-déjeuner.

So-see-suh

Bread	Pain
I bought the **bread** this morning.	J'ai acheté le **pain** ce matin.

Pein

As you know, you will find bakeries in almost every French village, where you can order the most famous French bread, "la baguette".

Of course, you will also find pastries, "pâtisseries" and "viennoiseries", such as "croissants" and "pain au chocolat", to enjoy your breakfast.

As for bread, it is a tradition in France to always have some in the middle of the table, for people to share during their meal. Most of the time, it is a "baguette", or a similar type of bread.

Chicken	Poulet
That **chicken** is raw.	Ce **poulet** est crû.

Poo-leh

Pancakes	Pancakes
These **pancakes** are fluffy.	Ces **pancakes** sont moelleux.

Pan-keh-kes

Rice	Riz
The **rice** is ready.	Le riz est prêt

Ree

Beef	Boeuf
The flavor of the **beef** is delicious.	La saveur du **boeuf** est délicieuse.

Beh-kon

The French, like Italian and Spanish people, eat a lot of red meat and have the best recipes to make it melt in your mouth. Hungry yet?

Milk	Lait
I think this **milk** has gone bad.	Je crois que ce **lait** n'est plus bon.

Leh

Cake	Gâteau
You can eat more **cake**.	Tu peux manger plus de **gâteau**.

Gah-toh

Soup	Soupe
This **soup** is hot.	Cette **soupe** est chaude.

Soo-puh

"Onion soup" is a famous dish in France, mostly served as a starter.

Onion	Onion
I was chopping **onions**.	Je découpais des **onions**.

Oh-nee-on

Garlic	Ail
You need to add **garlic** and stir.	Tu dois rajouter de l'**ail** et touiller.

Ah-ee

Garlic, onions and olive oil, are often used in French dishes, especially southern ones!

Lemon	Citron
These **lemons** look very nice.	Ces **citrons** ont l'air très bons.

C-trohn

Orange	Orange

| I want **orange** juice, please. | J'aimerais du jus d'orange, s'il-vous plaît. |

Oh-ran-guh

| Peanut | Cacahuète |
| I am allergic to **peanuts**. | Je suis allergique aux **cacahuètes**. |

Kah-Kah-oo-ett

"Cacahuète" is an important one. It is, after all, one of the most common food allergies.

We are almost done with this first level!

Just one more conversation! Let's go!

Veronica: *I am hungry.*

J'ai faim.

Karol: *Let's see. There are still eggs, cheese and bread from breakfast.*

Voyons voir. Il y a encore des oeufs, du fromage et du pain du petit-déjeuner.

Veronica: *Uhm... Do we have potatoes and onions? They can be good with eggs.*

Uhm... Est-ce que nous avons des patates et des onions? Ce serait bien avec les oeufs.

Karol: *No. I could not go grocery shopping yesterday.*

Non. Je n'ai pas pu aller faire les courses hier.

Veronica: *It is fine. Maybe I could go to the bakery by the corner.*

C'est pas grave. Peut-être que je pourrais aller à la boulangerie, à l'angle.

Karol: *I don't think it is open today.*

Je ne crois pas que ce soit ouvert aujour'dhui.

Veronica: *Oh... I could go for a piece of beef, then. The brasserie next door offers take away meals. They're delicious. Do you want anything?*

116

Oh... j'aurais bien envie d'une côte de boeuf, alors. La brasserie d'à côté propose des plats à emporter. Ils sont délicieux. Tu veux quelque-chose?

Karol: *That sounds nice! Can you get me a niçoise salad?*

Bonne idée! Tu peux me prendre une salade niçoise ?

Veronica: *Sure! Anything else?*

Bien-sûr! Tu veux autre chose?

Karol: *Maybe some sparkling water. They should have Perrier.*

Peut-être un peu d'eau pétillante. Ils devraient avoir du Perrier.

Veronica: Sounds fine. I will be back soon.

D'accord. Je reviens bientôt.

I hope it wasn't too difficult as food is very important. Do you agree?

Conclusion

C ongratulations, you've made it! See, it wasn't too hard, was it?

As you realized by now, this wasn't your typical language book. If you tried and failed to learn French in the past, you now discovered a new approach, one that you can build on to take your French adventure to the next level. In going away from formal vocabulary and grammar lessons, together we shifted your focus from 'learning' French, to 'speaking' French. Two very different things!

More than just the "rules" of French grammar, today you have a sense of "the soul and music" of the French language. You built a true solid foundation in French and, even if you don't realize it yet, you are now capable of navigating social situations, create connections, keep contacts, as well as make friends. As I mentioned at the start, what's the point in knowing grammatical rules if you can't order your own food!

I won't bore you with the reasons why being able to speak another language is a huge benefit for you. Or why French in particular will open a world of opportunities. I'm sure you're already convinced! But learning a new language is indeed a complex and rich experience, making this book a journey – your journey – into a new culture.

A beautiful culture you're now a part of.

No one is ever 'ready', so get out there! Travel, read fiction and newspapers in French, watch films, eat French foods, make French friends, and immerse yourself in French-speaking cultures. Sure, you'll make a few mistakes at first. But who cares! You can always go back through our lessons and keep building your confidence. I'm sure you'll get there in no time.

This is just the first volume of this series, all packed full of vocabulary and dialogs, covering essential, everyday French that will ensure you master the basics.

You can find the rest of the books in the series, as well as a whole host of other resources, at LearnLikeNatives.com. Simply add the book to your library to take the next step in your language learning journey. If you are ever in need of new ideas or direction, refer to our 'Speak Like a Native' eBook, available to you for free at LearnLikeNatives.com, which clearly outlines practical steps you can take to continue learning any language you choose.

A language should be lived, not just learned. So learn it, live it and, most importantly, enjoy it!

www.LearnLikeNatives.com

Learn Like a Native is a revolutionary **language education brand** that is taking the linguistic world by storm. Forget boring grammar books that never get you anywhere, Learn Like a Native teaches you languages in a fast and fun way that actually works!

As an international, multichannel, language learning platform, we provide **books, audio guides and eBooks** so that you can acquire the knowledge you need, swiftly and easily.

Our **subject-based learning**, structured around real-world scenarios, builds your conversational muscle and ensures you learn the content most relevant to your requirements.
Discover our tools at *LearnLikeNatives.com*

When it comes to learning languages, we've got you covered!